Spirit Animal Lessons

poems by

Brenda Galloway Conway

Finishing Line Press
Georgetown, Kentucky

Spirit Animal Lessons

ACKNOWLEDGMENTS

Special thanks to Kristin, Erin, Athena, Dani, Linda, Chrissy and Marcia

Publisher: Leah Huete de Maines
Editor: Christen Kincaid
Cover Artist: Kristin Smith
Cover Photographer/Digitizer: Erin Stricker
Author Photo Photographer: Athena Nurton
Cover Design: Elizabeth Maines McCleavy

Order online: www.finishinglinepress.com
also available on amazon.com

Author inquiries and mail orders:
Finishing Line Press
PO Box 1626
Georgetown, Kentucky 40324
USA

Contents

Winter Sister 1

Loss of Essence 2

Seeing 4

John 6

The Tree We Planted 8

Measuring Summer 9

My Old Skin 10

Better 11

Night Terrors 12

Two Cookies 13

The Shed 14

Blessing for Your Loss 15

Spirit Animal Lessons 16

Pink Sweater 17

Tornado 18

Fear of Swinging 19

House 20

October 21

Life Lace 22

Possibility Purloined 23

Sunday Morning 24

May 2, 2004 25

Unlikely 26

All Day 27

Driving Through Fog 28

Dedicated to Tim,
for your unwavering belief and support

Winter Sister

Winter sister
her purpose and beauty overlooked
her landscape still at best
brutal more often

She brought the death cycle
that was the catalyst
for another sister's bloom
and another's ripening
  even though the gift was shunned

But, even she, early on
was repulsed by her hollow sky
frightened of the jagged metal edge of her climate

Not so now
whether or no anyone else is

Her barren limbs raised
in tortured beauty
Her bitter cold the very power to gestate
her howling winds the mating call
beckoning change

That she feels her purpose
and cannot help but see her stark beauty
is enough

Loss of Essence

He really
has been dead for years
but his body remains; stubbornly in denial
Make no mistake,
the loss of his essence has
left his body worse for the wear—
  —confused mind
  —uncertain steps
  —frayed and severed relationships in pulpy heaps
You'd think anyone could see it if they looked; glanced even
Maybe it is just out of politeness that they participate in
his decades old delusion
or maybe out of lack of a reference point for what is expected
in situations of peopleless bodies
Slow suicide that you won't accept you have already committed
(because you are still committing it)
is thick and itchy—
a woolen sadness worn by those around you
But more leaden still
is the extravagance of waste
  —one, fresh, crisp, ripple chip out of the bag,
  the others abandoned
  left to go soggy and stale
  in a village of starving children
The tools were given
for a life respectful of the gift
yet, he,
time and time again
halfheartedly wrapped his hand around the grip
loosely
to assure the task would be performed awkwardly and then
let the handle fall, end over end, to the floor
banging his toe
and all the bare toes of those around him
  —toe Chopsticks with a claw hammer

Today
tenuously balancing my anger at what will be my final memories
of him against my memories of who he was when he lived
in his body
I prayed for his resurrection, for his salvation
But, I can't say if that prayer was for here
     —his body not strong enough to take him back from
     the look of it
or, for wherever awaits when his body finally realizes
and accepts
his abdication

Seeing

It used to be
That I saw through
eyes more innocent
      —corneas glazed with hope cells
Not so now
for I see that sometimes there is
no chance
for a happy ending;
no assurance that everything
no matter how brutal
will bring Sunday school good if you but let it

I cannot be soapbox sure
that it was not always this way—
perhaps it's that I was a reality virgin
believing in protection from pain
when truly there is none

But, now
I know no
sentinel—earthly or divine
stands between my soul and
the cross—cut shredder of seeing
without wavering
for I have seen him step to one side

My hope hymen
burst by the clumsy, savage penetration
of the changer rapist
      —and I cannot escape the day
      —or forget, or put it in a box on a memory shelf
      —or trust my old sight will come back
         (and more sagely)
     with time

I cannot hold hands with today for fear
it might be a shadow
or a disguise
or a mutation of that
one yesterday

I will suffocate rather than breathe out what little trust
is left in me
because I do not know
that there will be more to draw in
My eyes, the same
eyes that once shot out like
sparks from a welder
to find the good, to find the why
now furtively
search for the second shoe and the third
(for tragedies are three footed)

I used to throw my make it better
into a canyon
completely sure I would hear
the echo
            —faint as fog sound or sure as a train in
            your living room
            it did not matter the decibel
            only that I heard it as I knew I would

Now I fear that my sound
is absorbed before it finds its ear
            —a swimmer with no place to turn and push off at
            the end of the pool
The hope holocaust is here
my death camp rages behind the gray green of iris and pupil
and in front of lens and Visine whites
I stand when I long to lie
thin as epidermis
between

John

I first encountered you when I tried to park
next to your over the line crowding my space
car.
You were rifling around in the back seat
seemingly trying to find something.
I was irritated
even though I, too, am often a line crosser.
I pulled the nose of my car back out
and, regardless of the fact I got a better,
closer spot;
regardless that there were plenty of spots
I was cranky.
Then, we met again,
more closely but not formally
as we were entering the same
door;
which you clumsily but so
earnestly held open for me.
We even had the same woman
in charge of shortening our hair.
She cut yours first.
Made sense, you did not have much;
it would go faster.
She called you John.
I watched you in the chair—
something was bruising your mind
but, nonetheless, you showed interest in those around you
not self-absorbed; not a man who would be angry
about a parking spot.
Your face is broad and friendly though I can't help
but notice the sadness
hiding behind your cheeks, next to your ears.
"Wow John, your hair is really long!"
But it is only the length of two pieces of rice
placed end to end.

"I know, I know. I've just…been busy, haven't had time."
The story behind why you haven't had time
is at the center of your slight slump in the chair
but you don't tell it
instead letting the hairdresser talk about the recent loss
of her father.
In those fifteen minutes
I realized I am not the person I would like to be;

I am not you, John.
I wanted to apologize, sincerely, for my behavior
regarding the parking spot
but you were not even aware of the slight
and I let you walk right past me
back out the door
without saying one word.

The Tree We Planted

the breeze brings my dad
in choke cherry confetti
I smile and miss him

Measuring Summer

The life cycle of summer
is not measured in
hours or days or months;
it is measured in corn.
When summer is young and playful,
it busies itself with a game of
tug-of-war against the ground,
soon tiring of the distraction and skipping away;
leaving bright green, frayed ends of
cornstalks sticking up in the playground.
When summer is older and
about the serious business of
introducing bees to marigolds and catmint,
corn is busy practicing
perfect posture in deep green,
whispering to summer of shorter days
and cooler nights to come.
Sun-bleached flattops on the cornfields
under a sky sagging with the weight of
stars and heat
bring melancholy
as summer smells its mortality
mixed with honeysuckle;
so many nestlings never hatched,
so many shoulders never burned.
In the end, corn's fruit is
clumsily cleaved leaving
stalks to the reaper
while summer sits on autumn's front porch—
but only in the afternoon
waiting to die with fallen leaves around her feet.

My Old Skin

To some, I suppose, it is like wet crepe paper—
thin and blotchy and folded on itself…
but I love my old skin better than any skin I've ever worn
In the folds and wrinkles
are tucked years of living learning
   —some things useless to me now as a push up bra but,
   mine nonetheless
In the age spots and kaleidoscope complexion
are the smells of wood smoke and camphor,
the warmth of a ripe, vine strawberry and forgotten hot flashes

I concern myself no more with the world's pursuit of pretty
and am glad of it
I concern myself with hummingbird nectar, garage sales, lost
reading glasses
and the obituaries
Like the mockingbird in August, I have neither mate nor nest to
sing to protect
but, unlike him, I sing just the same

Seventy-six years of world war and men on the moon and lovers
   and jump ropes and a husband buried too soon
hang from my bones
and I have never been so comfortable as in my old skin

Better

I stand by
a tall window
that holds August
outside;
nowhere to run despair and
recently treated for fleas
brown carpet
inside (not my cat)
I realize
for the first time
I deserve better—
everyone
deserves better—
than this
My three-year-old son
plays in a patch of
sunshine that pushed
through the curtains;
backlit, stalagmite hair
Who will he become?
Will he be you
like you are your father
only worse with the
strength of another generation?
Can knowing we deserve
better
free us?
Keep us safe?

Night Terrors

I have interlocked my stare
first hand, up close
with the snake-jaw-wide,
frozen brown eyes
of the third deer
        the first already beyond the far ditch
        the second, clipped but still upright
There was time to stop, time to turn;
a possible path to take her away from the hungry maw of
sight searing headlights and an insatiable bumper
    my brakes had done all they could do to counter
    blood and fur laced impact
In deer fashion, her path irreversible once hoof hit blacktop,
that uneven, sliding tapping that forced forward movement
I held her terror too intimately in my sight
I smelled it
and death
seeping through
the cracking windshield

Two Cookies

You came to me soft and warm
    —bread out of the oven
      buttered with hold your breath wonder

      —Butterfly on my finger
scared to even blink for fear
you'd mount the wind and ride away

A rabbit in a hawk-shaped cloud shadow cast by the past,
I wanted to run but
my safe place—no bramble or hole
      you—always you

Like cookies in an oven
our edges melted together creating a new shape
that is better

Your gift
      yielding and metronome steady;
a quiet dawn strong enough to hold the sky and me

Time's magician hands will not bring decay and wistful echoes
      of what was but, like a child's Christmas anticipation,
the promise of just what we wanted
      and all the things we didn't know we wanted and
      a porch swing (for rocking chairs sit too far apart)
The age spots of my hands held in the acceptance and
work-scarred, thinning skin of yours

The Shed

The shed her plank and nail twin
so shed like on the outside
unless you notice the whimsical line of vine
and the confetti toss of story-flag-guards that refuse to be
relegated to the inside
or the sleeve-wiped mustard on the lock
     errant but playful and beckoning

To open the door is to feel the magic and surprise;
     sun sequins bouncing off of water
     nesting-bowl-stacked with
lullaby lilt, summer night sounds
A suitable haven for lawn mowers and dreams;
     secrets and hopes in hidden envelopes shelved with
     wasp spray
Unanticipated but perfect in its patchwork of
irrepressible colors
Spider and egg sack hostile
Lean on me friendly
Ready for an impromptu garden party on metal chairs
or the serious business of rake storage

Blessing for Your Loss

May your pain—
        uncooked spaghetti brittle
        glass shard sharp
give way to memories
        smiling from old pictures
        winking from cherished objects
        woven ravelproof in the frayed fabric
                of your soul
May your tears
starting and stopping like a new driver on a clutch
leak all of the coulda, shoulda, woulda out of you
to make room for the quiet, unexpected knowledge
that love, life and death are perfectly imperfect
        and that's okay
May you receive the gift of
        "I'm still with you"
whispered in the rustle of leaves on concrete
dancing above the smell of pan-fried chicken
or in the hide 'n seek words of a check-out-line stranger
        meant just for you
May family, friends and ice cream
be there for you when you need them and
        also when you don't

And may you grieve with the
        same bloodless knuckle determination
        and courage that it will take to feel better

Spirit Animal Lessons

Take-off and landing
wrong size shoes awkward, clumsy
At home navigating wind currents
not tree branches or telephone pole tops,
never whole in the absence of motion
...but sometimes watching and resting
are frustratingly necessary

In pursuit of nourishment,
the folded plummet to the ground
worth the chance of earth collision
to capture what is needed
to be sustained

Hickory-brown mottled white feathers
is what the earthbound see;

Watered down walnut broken abruptly
by fanned, heated rust
is what the sun smells rising toward it;

Freedom to slide across
the wind,
exhilaration,
strength and authenticity,
purpose
is what the hawk tastes

Pink Sweater

I have seen you.
You stand to the left of a white and gray
flecked tile hall near a room that holds
your things and has for nearly a year.
Yet, every minute of every day
this place is a surprise to you—
more unfamiliar with each short, stiff step
and you take hundreds every day
restlessly moving toward or away from
something only you know.
Countless hours spent tugging at the bottom
of your pink sweater
fretting with string that once held a
pearl button
determined to understand what it is and
why it is
knowing once you did
not knowing you never will again

Tornado

E5 C&I
Head on collision
Nature crossed the center line
Tardy response—
    futile jerk of the steering wheel to one side
Impact so cacophonous—
    it's heard by a million hearts
Manmade and nature spawned
    in heaps—
    an old lady's junk drawer
Geographic Alzheimer's
Time has a paint brush but no eraser

Fear of Swinging

I wish I were the
go-down-swinging type
but
I'm not
I'm the
hope the pitcher is no good
or has a sore arm
type
Standing at the plate
afraid to swing and miss
      to embarrass myself
      disappoint my cheering squad
While I have the bat in my hand,
and before I've swung and missed,
THREE times,
I can still believe I can hit a home run
If I swing and miss
I cannot
My most fervent hope
  my only chance for "success"
merely the advancement
of one base—a walk—
built on another's
"failure"
At least she threw the ball

House

Sunken and sullen
Weighted down by years
and neglect
How many families filled your
rooms?
How many Christmas trees stood
looking out of your window?
Show me your secrets
Whisper the memories you hold
in the paint specks, layered
wallpaper and gray plank floors
Who planted the iris by the steps?
Whose rusty bike is patiently
waiting on what is left of the
back porch?
What love and laughter
tears and anger splashed
against the walls and filled
the cubby holes which now
hold only silence and cobwebs?
Who built the fires in the winters
and whose bodies were caressed
by a breeze from an open window
all of those hot summer nights?
Did the smell of bread baking and
coffee and card games beckon
from the kitchen?
How many babies drew their first
breath and how many men their
last cradled under your plaster
and lathe ceilings?
And who left you here to die
raped of windows and doors
with only a half dead tree
to comfort you?

October

October rips off the veil
demands to be seen for who she is
Proud to be Leah, not Rachel
Let Jacob have the uniform green of summer;
that which is thought to be better, prettier, more desirable
He does not deserve this level of honesty
She drops all that is not her, not necessary
in fractured yellow perfection under the maple tree
and haphazard crimson under the sumac;
sending robins and hummingbirds,
impatiens and boats to their rooms
She takes up painting
    with frost crystals on rocks and car windows
      delicate brutality that bonfires
      cannot stave off
    and in the curled tawny of brittle oak leaves—
    broad, impasto brushstrokes over the wind canvas
She delights in the capricious—
short sleeve warm in the afternoon, flannel cold at night
hot chocolate cool in the mornings
Her voice
    a whisper for so long
sings an aria
of squirrels rattling leaves
chainsaws
geese calling
ending in a crescendo of doorbell chimes
and a Trick or Treat chorus

Life Lace

I have lately thought
if I could remove from my memory's sight
all of the hard things,
the sad things,
the disappointing things,
the bad choices
(mine and
the ones of those charged with my care);
I would be left with a bolt of irregular lace
  —the kind you can buy at WalMart
  for pennies on the dollar
  due to the mismatched,
  sideways nature of the pattern
This life lace,
prone to yellowing and stiffness,
is still adequate
for christening blankets, wedding dresses
and Thanksgiving tablecloths more dedicated
to Braille texture than perfect pattern

Possibility Purloined

It is assumed, willed even, that loss
is a violent ripping of the
fabric of your reality;
a denial of future memories;
a light that goes out
in the window of the past

But what is loss,
how is it held in your
hand to be examined or
in your heart to suck all the juices out
when loss is about what never was
and, now, never can be

Sunday Morning

We lie
> (your arm under the curve of my neck
> my hair, wound around it, tugged but not pulled
> my leg across the crease above
> your perpetually taut thigh)
in the deep hammock
of Sunday morning
The indoor sky—leaf shadow mottled like a sycamore trunk
is all that meets our
sleepy eyes
The air around us light,
not laboring under the weight of last night taco smells or
the bonfire leftovers holding tight to your stocking cap
that often hangs on the bed post
Our unhurried words
wander away
to play tumble with the white noise
drone of a lawn mower
In this moment
the moon marble center of perfection
sighs deeply and roundly,
content

May 2, 2004

The scene haunting,
an Andrew Wyeth painting,
as I look back down the slanted boat dock
at your slumped shoulders—
still moving up and down
to the rhythm
of ashes-in-the-waves-forever-goodbye
The water which cleaved you together
now separates you;
him below and you above,
your feet
skimming the surface,
his tugged by the current

Unlikely

I hate starlings,
Poe association aside
They are base birds
     water ballooning the driveway with thin,
     digested juniper berries,
     unkempt and half-hearted nests spilling from
     under the grill lid…again
     suet thieving bully birds
Akin to a possum with an overbite and the mange
as far as redeeming qualities go

But, on a late winter afternoon
a flock undulated into the sky
in synchronized swimming fashion
The slanted sun sliced between
stubby, blunt wings
shapeshifting them into iridescent knife blades
splayed out over a scrap of cerulean sky
Momentary angels on earth

All Day

They say you do this all day,
that you don't know what you're saying,
that you are fine, not to worry
    —as if this dismisses their indifference—
They pass your room with as
much attention as they would pay a
soft breeze or a distant bird's call;
noticed, not important
But the sound clawing its way
under your door and into the hallway,
neither soft nor distant,
is the sound of terror
    —a forlorn and bewildered siren—
you call for your mama
dead now for over thirty years
and, when she doesn't come
to chase the shadows and
hold your sharp, thin shoulders
in her monster slayer arms,
your voice climbs the stairs
to hysteria
and still
not she, not anyone
comes
but you do this all day
they can't come every time

Driving Through Fog

Winter midnight still, painted gray
yielding and ghost kiss cold
The familiar becomes an adventure
    to the thrill seeker
a tranquility bandit
    to the timid
Over anticipated curves
The old water tower half recognized
geographic bewilderment
false detour
CONCENTRATE! Concentrate on where you are
no room for the round ripe taste of the destination
The road has not changed
trees did not uproot and migrate,
road signs stand true, albeit abrupt
Out of focus beauty for those
who would see it
Trust, cloud traveler
leave your wake as you cleave the mist

Brenda Galloway Conway is a life-long Midwesterner. She currently lives in the Ozarks with her husband and the flying squirrels that visit most nights. She writes poetry, short stories and children's books. Brenda loves small towns, nonprofits and nature.

Spirit Animal Lessons is Brenda's first poetry chapbook. This collection of poetry explores the nuances of grief, aging, the challenges of striving to be a better person and nature.

She was a recent semifinalist for her humorous story *Call Your Mama* in Tulip Tree Publishing's Humor Story Contest. Brenda's poetry was chosen for the 2023 Detroit Lakes Flowerpot Poetry Festival which melds literary art and public art into a temporary, accessible art walk. Brenda is most interested in the pivot point that changes a person forever; whether that is in a barely noticeable way or a whole-life shake up.

www.ingramcontent.com/pod-product-compliance
Lightning Source LLC
Chambersburg PA
CBHW022057080426
42734CB00009B/1385